Heart-Shaped
PICKLES

By Karla Wheeler

Dedicated to anyone
who has ever felt sad
following the death
of someone dear.

© 2003 by Karla Wheeler

Other grief support books and booklets
by Karla Wheeler include:

Timmy's Christmas Surprise
Afterglow: Signs of Continued Love
Afterglow for Bereaved Families

All rights reserved. No part of this book may be reproduced without prior permission of the publisher. Printed in the United States of America.

Published By:

Quality of Life Publishing Co., Naples, Florida

Quality of Life Publishing Co. specializes in clinical and grief support publications for hospices and other end-of-life care organizations. Publishers of *Quality of Life Matters,*™ an end-of-life care publication for physicians and other clinicians.

1-877-513-0099 (toll free in U.S. and Canada)
1-239-513-9907 (phone)
1-239-513-0088 (fax)

www.QoLpublishing.com

ISBN 0-9675532-2-9

Library of Congress Control Number: 2003094197

Based on a true story,
Heart-Shaped Pickles
is published in loving
memory of Jenny's
grandfathers, who died
four weeks apart in the
spring of 1998.

We hope this book
will touch your heart
in gentle ways.

G iggly. That's how Jenny felt whenever she played with her grandfathers. She felt all giggly and warm inside.

Grampa Dutch would scoop her up into his big, strong arms, and they would play their favorite game: "Find Grampa's Hair."

Grampa had been bald for many, many years, which is what made this special game so much fun. "Okay, Jenny Lee," Grampa would say, "find Grampa's hair."

Jenny would work hard to make

Jenny would search and search for even ONE hair on Grampa's bald head!

her face look serious, just like a detective trying to solve an important mystery. "Hmmm...." she would mutter as she studied every inch of Grampa's smooth head, searching for even *one* hair!

In the most surprised-sounding

voice she could muster, little Jenny would announce, "I *found* it! *Here's* Grampa's hair!" Then her tiny fingers would tickle the hairs of his bushy eyebrows. Grampa's face would light up brighter than the morning sun, and his eyes would shine with love.

Jenny's pigtails would start wiggling from all the giggling.

Whenever Jenny visited Grandpa Wheeler in Canada, they played a different game. "Find Grampa's Hair" was just too boring, because Grandpa Wheeler had lots of thick, wavy, silver hair. So they made up their own

Grandpa Wheeler had lots of hair (except on his forehead). He liked to play "Wink, Wink."

special giggle game, which they called "Wink, Wink."

Jenny always wanted her grandpa to go first. Grandpa Wheeler would wink in a pattern, and Jenny would try to wink back in the same pattern.

Left eye wink once,
* right eye wink once,*
Left eye three times,
* right eye three times,*
Right eye once,
* left eye once... Now repeat...*

Jenny usually started out perfectly. But matching wink for wink, sooner or later, she would get confused. Her face would scrunch up on the left side, then on the right side. Finally, Jenny would laugh so hard she couldn't wink at all.

Spending time with Grandpa Wheeler and Grampa Dutch was one of her most favorite things to do in the whole wide world.

When Jenny was five years old, both grandfathers got very sick. The doctors and nurses did everything they could to help each of them get well again. But the grandpas had lived a long, long time, and the diseases they battled could not be cured.

Sadly, one day in April, Grampa Dutch died. Only a few weeks later, in early May, Grandpa Wheeler died, too.

Jenny no longer felt giggly at all. She felt very sad. She knew she would never again play "Find Grampa's Hair" with Grampa Dutch or "Wink, Wink" with Grandpa Wheeler.

Jenny felt even worse when she saw how very, very sad her Mom and Dad had become. Dad usually shared interesting nature and science facts with her. But not now. Mom usually smiled a lot and hummed happy tunes. But not now.

At lunchtime one Saturday, three glum faces sat around the kitchen table. "I miss my grandpas," Jenny said softly.

"So do I, sweetie," Mom whispered,

as she gave Jenny's hand a gentle squeeze. Dad didn't say anything, but Jenny saw a tear trickle down his cheek, just below his eyeglasses.

Dad tried to change the subject by passing Jenny the jar of crinkle-cut pickle slices. "Here, Jenny-Benny," he said in a voice meant to sound upbeat. "Let's have a contest to see who can eat the most pickles."

Mom wrinkled up her nose and mumbled, "yuck." She didn't like pickles and could never understand how her family could eat an entire jar at one sitting.

As Jenny's fork grabbed the first pickle slice, she let out a giggle. She placed the pickle on her plate and jabbed her fork into the jar once again. Then she let out another giggle.

She held her fork high to show her parents what she had discovered. Drip, drip, drip went the pickle juice onto the tablecloth. Mom and Dad frowned at the wet mess on the table.

"Look at this cute little heart-shaped pickle!" Jenny exclaimed, twirling the fork around so she could admire the pickle from every possible angle. "See? It's in the shape of a beautiful heart! I knew it, I just *knew* it!! Now I'm *sure* my grandpas are together, and they still love me — and *all* of us!"

Whenever Jenny got excited, she would begin talking non-stop. And now she barely paused to take a breath between sentences as she told her parents about her discoveries.

Ever since her grandfathers died, she'd been seeing hearts everywhere she looked.

While riding on the school bus Monday, Jenny said, she was thinking about her grandpas because the new bus driver was bald just like Grampa Dutch, and he winked at her just like Grandpa Wheeler used to do.

As she gazed out the window of the bus, she saw two fluffy heart-shaped clouds in the sky. They looked so light, so bright, and so free as they slowly floated by.

"Seeing those clouds made me feel

like Grampa Dutch and Grandpa Wheeler were still with me," Jenny said happily.

Then, during morning recess that same day, Jenny found two heart-shaped pieces of mulch on the playground. "I've been keeping them with me," she added, reaching into her pocket. "Wanna see?"

Jenny carefully placed two pieces of playground mulch on the table, right next to the drippy pickle spots.

No one spoke. Three pairs of eyes stared at the wood chunks.

Jenny took a deep breath and swallowed hard.

Dad's dark eyes had that special softness they get when he's pleased about something. Mom's green eyes were watery, but she was grinning, so Jenny continued talking a mile a minute. She told her parents about all kinds of heart-shaped things she had found.

For instance, a few days ago at a friend's birthday party, she ate at least fifteen heart-shaped potato

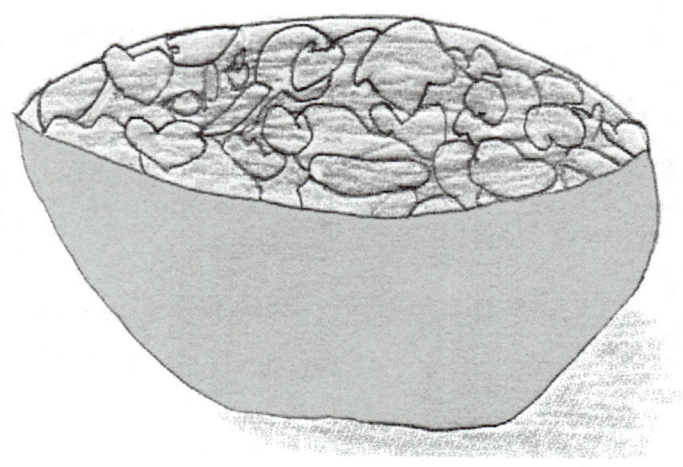

chips. There might have been many more heart-shaped chips in the bowl, Jenny noted, but she lost count when her tummy got full.

Yesterday at the neighborhood park, Jenny romped around in hundreds of heart-shaped leaves that had fallen from her favorite shade tree.

And last night while playing in the bubble bath, she was delighted to watch how all the teensy bubbles stuck together in blobs that formed really cool heart designs.

Jenny grinned. "Everywhere I look now I see hearts!" Her big brown eyes widened. "And Mom... Dad... did you notice all those heart-shaped puddles on the driveway this morning when we got home from the store? There

must have been ten or eleven of them!"

With that, Jenny ran out the front door, calling for Mom and Dad to come, too. The three of them stood next to their red van, looking down at the puddles on the concrete. Jenny began to count. "Yep, eleven heart-shaped puddles," she confirmed.

Mom smiled. Dad smiled. And, of course, Jenny smiled, too.

"Let's go finish our lunch," Mom said, humming a happy tune as they walked back into the house.

"Speaking of puddles," Dad said with enthusiasm, "remind me to tell you about the amazing nature program I watched last night on rain forests."

As they settled back into their chairs at the table, Dad added, "But first, how about that pickle-eating

contest, Jenny-Benny?"

As Dad reached for the jar of pickles, Mom held out her hand, motioning for Dad to give *her* the pickles. Dad looked puzzled.

Mom placed the pickle jar smack dab in the center of the table, picked up her fork, and said in her warm, chipper way, "I have a *great* idea. Let's have a contest to see who can find the most heart-shaped pickles!"

Dad chuckled, and as three forks

moved toward the open jar, Dad stated with confidence, "twelve."

Mom asked cheerfully, "Twelve heart-shaped pickles? Is that your official prediction, dear?"

"No," Dad replied in his scientific voice. The thumb of his left hand began to scratch his chin, a sure sign that Dad was deep in thought. "Actually, I was thinking about puddles, not pickles. I'm certain I counted twelve — not eleven — heart-shaped puddles on the driveway just now."

Jenny was the first one to start giggling, then Mom, then Dad. The room glowed with warmth and love as three giggly people sat at the kitchen table, busily counting pickle slices on their plates.

And how many heart-shaped pickles did each of them find?

Well, that's for *you* to decide!

THE END

Resources

---

*For Parents,
Teachers,
Counselors,
and Other
Grownups*

Discussion Guide

Here are some suggestions for engaging the thoughts and feelings of children as you share this book with them.

Pages 1-5: Jenny loved to play giggle games with her grandpas. Give an example of a favorite game or activity you enjoyed with your special person who died.

Pages 6-7: Jenny's Mom and Dad were so sad after the grandfathers died that they forgot how to smile. Have people around you ever been that sad? In what ways could you help a sad person remember that it's normal to be sad, but it's also normal — and important — to laugh and have fun, too?

Pages 12-13: The bus driver reminded Jenny of her grandfathers. Reminders of our special person can come in all kinds of ways. What reminds you of your special person?

Pages 12-18: Whenever Jenny saw heart-shaped objects, she believed these were signs from her grandpas that their love for her was still very much a part of her life. Give examples of objects or experiences that have been meaningful to you.

Overall: What do you think are some of the feelings Jenny might have been experiencing at different times in the story? How about Mom? And Dad?

Just for Fun: How many heart-shaped pickles do you think Jenny found? Mom? Dad? If Jenny and her parents were sitting here with you right now, what heart-shaped items do you think they might see?

8 Things Kids Can Teach Grownups About Grief

By Karla Wheeler

My husband and I were emotionally devastated when our fathers died just four weeks apart in the spring of 1998. It was our young daughter, Jenny, who helped us to smile again, thanks to her childlike approach to grief, which I've chronicled in *Heart-Shaped Pickles*. Through my years as a hospice volunteer, I had often seen similar situations, where children brought comfort to others in sweet, heartwarming ways. I began developing a list of things kids might be able to teach *us* about death and loss.

Susan McMahan, Psy.D., a children's grief counselor at Hospice of Naples in Florida, agrees that young children have a natural, uninhibited approach to grief. "As the story in *Heart-Shaped Pickles* illustrates," Dr. McMahan says, "children grieve in simple, straightforward ways. Sometimes a childlike approach to the grieving process can help all of us."

I am very grateful to Dr. McMahan for bringing her professional insights to the following examples of things children can teach grownups about grief.

1. NO SECRETS, PLEASE!

Raised in a death-denying society, we adults often muddle through grief, walking on eggshells, afraid to talk about it for fear of upsetting others, especially children. Dr. McMahan says it's best to have open communication with children. "Be honest, brief, clear, and heartfelt," she advises. "Kids don't try to hide the truth or sugar-coat it, so let's learn from them and keep the lines of communication open."

2. KISS IT & MAKE IT BETTER?

Children seem to understand that grief is a process, not an event. Unlike adults who might feel compelled by society to try to "fix it" when someone is grieving, children seem to understand that grief isn't fixable. Healing from a loss takes time. We can ease the way for each other one conversation at a time, one hug at a time, and one kiss at a time!

3. IT'S NOT FAIR!

Feelings of anger and guilt are normal and healthy when grieving, as are tears, and kids seem to show their feelings much more readily than grownups. Dr. McMahan points out, "No feeling is a bad feeling. Even anger is okay if we learn to express it in safe ways." Crying is okay for children *and* adults, she notes, because "tears let the pain out."

4. IT HURTS LESS WHEN SHARED

Kids' natural inclination is to give comfort to those who mourn and to accept comfort from others. By the time we're grownups, we've often lost touch with that natural process. If you are bereaved, don't hesitate to let friends and neighbors know how they can help you in specific ways, both practical and emotional.

5. FLOWERS ARE NICE & ICE CREAM, TOO!

Rituals can help ease the way, and kids seem to rise above society's expectations of appropriate expressions of grief. For instance, if placing flowers on a loved one's gravesite on birthdays and anniversaries is part of your ritual, you might ask your children what else to do that day to remember your special person. Don't be surprised if they suggest something non-traditional, like mint chocolate chip ice cream for dessert, because it was your loved one's favorite sweet treat!

6. I NEED MY BLANKIE!

Children love their "lovies." Whether it's a blankie or teddy bear, during stressful times, such items bring an extra sense of security. It's normal for adults to also want to keep a significant item nearby, such as a shirt, ring, book, or other object that helps us feel connected to our loved one. Dr. McMahan says that these "transitional items" can be just as comforting for grownups as for kids.

7. GIGGLES ARE GOOD

"There are no right or wrong ways to grieve," Dr. McMahan says. Some families might keep the memories of their loved one alive by watching funny home-movie footage, while others might volunteer at the animal shelter, because grandpa loved pets. Do whatever feels right to your family. But remember that grief doesn't always need to be somber and serious. Let's learn from our kids and give ourselves permission to also laugh and have fun in celebration of our loved one's life.

8. HEART-SHAPED PICKLES

As the story in this book illustrates, children are wonderfully open to signs of continued love following someone's death. We grownups often yearn for a sign that our loved one is okay. But are we searching too hard? Perhaps we can learn from children that a sign of continued love might be as simple as a heart-shaped cloud or pickle!

Hospice Can Help

If you or someone you know is bereaved, please consider contacting your local hospice. Many hospice and palliative care organizations offer free grief support programs to members of the community, including children's workshops conducted at local schools and churches.

To locate a hospice near you:

In the U.S.:

Contact the National Hospice & Palliative Care Organization. Website: www.nhpco.org; phone: 703-837-1500.

In Canada:

Contact the Canadian Palliative Care Association. Website: www.cpca.net; phone 800-668-2785.

About the Author: Gentle Grief Support

Author Karla Wheeler with photos of her "two dear Dads."

The first 20 years of KARLA WHEELER's publishing career seemed rather typical for a print journalist: newspaper reporter and editor, magazine editor, and editor of national medical journals.

But in 1998, Karla's writing path took an unexpected turn, following the back-to-back deaths of her beloved father and father-in-law. Her "two dear Dads," as she affectionately refers to them, died just four weeks apart, each of a different lingering illness.

Months later, Karla emerged from the depths

of grief with a strong social mission as a journalist: to help ease the way for those who grieve.

Heart-Shaped Pickles, which chronicles her family's bereavement experience, is Karla's third book on grief. She is also the author of *Afterglow: Signs of Continued Love,* a compilation of stories of comforting coincidences from those who grieve; and *Timmy's Christmas Surprise,* an uplifting story about a family grieving the death of their cat, Timmy. (Visit www.QoLpublishing.com to learn more.)

Karla has been a hospice volunteer since 1990, visiting with terminally ill patients and providing bereavement support to families. She and her husband, Gerry, live in Naples, Florida, with their daughter, Jenny.

Jenny, who is the illustrator of *Heart-Shaped Pickles* as well as *Timmy's Christmas Surprise,* continues to see hearts in unexpected ways!

How to Order

Quality of Life Publishing Co. specializes in gentle grief support books and booklets for readers of all ages. Here's how to order *Heart-Shaped Pickles* and other publications:

WEB SITE: www.QoLpublishing.com
Purchase online using your Visa, MasterCard, Discover, or American Express card.

EMAIL: books@QoLpublishing.com

PHONE: 1-877-513-0099
Toll-free in the U.S. and Canada
or call 1-239-513-9907

FAX: 1-239-513-0088

MAIL: Quality of Life Publishing Co.
P.O. Box 112050
Naples, FL 34108-1929

*DISCOUNTS. Be sure to ask about **substantial discounts** available to hospices and other grief support organizations.*